*THE

★ NITTY

GRITTY

GUIDEBOOK

A Guide To Greatness

The
Nitty
Gritty
Guidebook

Adrienne Bulinski and William V. Anderson

Illustrations by:
Adrienne Bulinski
Madison Rosel
Roselyn McDonald

Contact Be Known

To book Adrienne & Bill for school assemblies, retreats, student-athlete summits, student council conferences, workshops, conferences or any other gathering:

ab@adriennebulinski.com
adriennebulinski.com

Formatting and cover design by Adrienne Rosel Bulinski
Illustrations by Adrienne Rosel Bulinski

Guest illustrations by
Madison Rosel – p. 4; 39
Roselyn McDonald – p. 8; 27; 61; 67; 89

First Printing: Feb. 15, 2020

Paperback ISBN-13: 978-0-9978990-3-0
Ebook ISBN: 978-0-9978990-4-7

Library of Congress Control Number: 2020901168

Published by Be Known LLC
Arvada, CO 80007
U.S.A.

Special discounts are available on quantity purchases by schools, corporations, associations, educators, and others. For details, contact the publisher at ab@adriennebulinski.com

U.S. trade bookstores and wholesalers: please contact Be Known LLC at ab@adriennebulinski.com

Reviews and praise

"If you have spent any time around Adrienne, you immediately realize that she is a dynamo who is committed to young people. She cares about each person she encounters and leaves a little bit of herself (and gum!) with the audience every time she speaks. I know that she has poured so much of herself into this guidebook, because she has persevered so much in her own life. Read, Enjoy, Cherish. This is going to be great!" *-B. Elliot Hopkins, National Federation of High School Sports, Director of Sports, Sanctioning and Student Services*

"I have had the pleasure to be influenced by Adrienne and she is truly an inspiration and a blessing to so many. Her messages and teaching are spot on and will take you to the next level of you moving forward on your goals, dreams and aspirations. Her dedication to youth is admirable!" *-Deb Hult, Core Trainings Co-Founder*

"I highly recommend that you read Adrienne's *Nitty Gritty Guidebook*. It has been my privilege to have her as a speaker for the Ohio High School Athletic Association Student Leadership Conference, the largest high school student athletic conference in the country. Adrienne speaks and writes about the key characteristics such as sportsmanship, ethics, and integrity through both modeling these characteristics and by demonstrating leadership, citizenship, positive social skills, and ethical conduct.

Adrienne is an excellent speaker on the big stage and her writings help to support other learned outcomes. Her message will make an impact on the individual and as a member of any group. She reinforces the desire to succeed and to excel, higher moral and ethical standards, self-discipline and emotional maturity, respect for the rights of others and for authority, and high ideals of fairness in all human relationships. In this light, I believe her message will benefit all who choose to read it." *-Harvey Alston, CEO Best, Inc., Coordinator the for the OHSAA Foundation Student Leadership Conference, NFHS-NSLS*

"Adrienne is a dynamic motivational speaker with a singing voice to match. I have had the pleasure of working with her at several state association events, and I must admit, every time I hear her speak, I am reminded how powerful grit and perseverance can be if channeled toward one's goals. Adrienne's story is the very definition of grit and perseverance, and that is something that we all need on our journey through this lifetime." -*Omari Pearson, Passion to Purpose Goal & Mind Mapping, Founder & President*

"I have never met someone so passionate and caring. Adrienne not only inspires students but motivates them to keep pushing forward. She is very passionate about helping young people persevere and reach for their dreams. Her life story allows students to see no matter what their setbacks are and no matter what people tell them; they can achieve whatever dreams they have." -*Belinda Apodaca, Teacher, Student Council Advisor, Rocky Ford High School*

"Adrienne gave one of the most powerful, meaningful messages I've heard in my 35 years as a high school principal. Her message is spot-on and presented in a way in which students follow every word. She is not just another pretty face presenting her story. She is giving her audiences life skills and insight on how to get from point A to point B." -*Mark Goodheart, Principal, Otis-Bison High School*

"We recently were blessed to have Adrienne address our junior and senior students at our annual retreat which kicks off our school year. Adrienne is an extremely engaging speaker who draws on life experiences and God's Word as she instructs and motivates young people to take the necessary steps toward personal success." -*Andrew Hasz, Superintendent, Faith Christian Academy*

"Adrienne truly has a gift to be able to connect with young people the way she does through humor, through song and through honest conversation. It was a privilege to watch her in action." -*Jack Maher, Jeffco Public Schools Multimedia Journalist*

Join Adrienne on your favorite social platform

Instagram – YouTube – Facebook – Twitter - LinkedIn
@AdrienneBulinski

To Riley, Sadie, Kelly, Spencer, Madison, Henry, Rozi, Jude
and Mrs. Tillman.

May you always dream BIG… *and go for it!*

Luck is when preparation meets opportunity.

-Seneca

Go back to the previous page and memorize the whole page.

The end.

Just kidding...

Table of Contents

Introduction

WooHOO! I just did a little happy dance because I know the growth you are about to experience is going to be HUGE. Why am I so confident? Because I'm going to take you through the very tools that have helped me step fully into my own life's purpose and dreams. I'm going to share with you my roadmap of how I have navigated my own obstacles and charged after my goals.

This guidebook was written for you, the dreamer! I wrote this with the intention that you too can have profound growth in your own life if you spend just five minutes a day working through the nuggets of gold and inspiration on the pages that are before you! I want you to live your best life. I know without a doubt **our world needs *you*.** Yes YOU! You were uniquely created, and I believe you have something extremely powerful within you that our world *needs*. Why do I believe this? Because otherwise you wouldn't be here.

My ten-year-old niece once asked me, "Auntie Adrienne, what do you do for work?"

"Well, Madison, I work with people all over the country helping them build their self-confidence and understand their value so they can live their dreams. Then I help them map out a plan to go after their dreams."

Madison was perplexed, "You mean not everyone knows their life has value?" She asked.

"Unfortunately, no."

"All people should understand everyone has a purpose," Madison said matter-of-factly.

There you have it… from the lips of a ten-year-old. **You. Have. PURPOSE!** Friends, you have a profound purpose for your life! Let's uncover it and get you off your butt and in pursuit of it!

For those of you whom I have not personally met by shaking your hand and looking into the whites of your eyeballs, let me introduce myself. My name is Adrienne Bulinski. I am a wife, a stepmom, a mountain biking singing diva who is also a motivational speaker, author, blogger and a girl trying to figure out the life hacks of adulting. I deliver inspiring programs and workshops around the globe that help people lean into their purpose. I am writing this guidebook in partnership with my friend who also doubles as my mentor and business partner. Bill Anderson is my number one adviser, editor and creative collaborator. He is a former professor at Louisiana State University (LSU), has directed conferences all over the world and regularly volunteers his time to make a difference in the lives of others. He is a husband, father, grandfather, theatre producer/designer genius, writer and has the patience of a saint (*he deals with me*). As you may guess there is a large age gap between the two of us which benefits *you* so you may receive content and ideas that are tested and proven across generations. These writings are a collaboration of the two of us. Our goal is to give you the best possible tools so you may tackle your obstacles and live your dreams.

It is important to note, we believe you need the stepstool of standing on your failures so you can grab ahold of **success as you have defined**

it for your life. One of the most important things I have learned thus far: **you cannot know success without tasting failure**. In fact, I have found that if you don't fail every so often then you aren't pushing yourself to know what you're capable of. But what about the failures that try to break you as a person? What about failures that try to ruin you emotionally, physically and spiritually? I've been there too, and while your life may or may not be that dramatic in description, I am going to address life's obstacles no matter what scale you use to measure them. Let me remind you: **people who are failures fall and stay down; people who are champions fall and rise again.**

No matter where you are in your life's journey. This guide will work for you. It is a guide you can use to get brutally and unapologetically honest with *yourself*. It is important to note this guide is interactive, which means I'm going to give you the map, but *you* must do the work. In the upcoming pages I'm going to ask you to write down your dreams, ideas, and obstacles. I'm also going to ask you to write your plans and make lists. **Do it.** Do it before you skip ahead. Take the time to develop yourself and not just try to get to the end. **If you want your destination you will only find it in your journey.**

As we begin breaking down barriers I want you to read and write as though no one will ever see the pages of this book. These are your pages to be bold, to be brave, and to be you! So get honest with yourself because honesty is the path to growth.

Without it sounding weird I want to you to know I love you and I am cheering for you!

Let's do this!

Adrienne (& Bill).

Gratitude

A grateful heart is a magnet for miracles.
-Vicki Becker

In order to level-up your life I first want to ground ourselves in gratitude. So often we get focused on what we want (which is what we don't yet have) and our blinders don't allow us to take inventory of the blessings we already possess.

My first car was an old white Ford Taurus. Impressive? What if I told you this car was so beat up there was no harm in leaving the keys in the ignition... overnight... because no one wanted to steal it? Not only was my Taurus as beautiful as an old woman shuffling down the halls of a hospital with her gown untied and flapping in the breeze, but this beauty sat through a hailstorm that delivered baseball and grapefruit sized hail... the car, not the woman.

I'm from Kansas where hail and tornados are no joke. After the storm, the Taurus was technically a totaled, unsalvageable, vehicle. This old beauty's life had come to an end, or so *I* thought. My parents saw a different opportunity.

Since the engine still worked, they decided to replace the windows and give it a second life. That Taurus became my first mode of mechanical transportation. At the time I was a junior in high school and my parents required good grades and 100% effort in all activities I was involved in – or the car was history. I also had to keep my car well maintained and respected if I was afforded the **privilege** of possessing the keys. Did I mention the air conditioner didn't work (and summers were consistently in the 100s)? The radio didn't work either, nor the tape deck (forget even having a CD player), which was a tragedy for a dramatic teenager. Yet, despite its flaws I was grateful I didn't have to walk or ride my bike.

Because I drove such a dump, I didn't understand why my dad insisted my car be washed and vacuumed every week. Sometimes wrinkle cream won't cover the old age and damage from the sun or storm.

Even when I washed my car, it still looked dirty due to the missing paint and hail damage. My dad's response, "be grateful for what you have and take care of what you have; otherwise, how do you expect to ever be blessed with more?"

As I would wash my beat-up hunk-of-junk I would contemplate his advice. I still do today.

It wasn't about the car. It never was. It was about being grounded in gratitude for what you have RIGHT NOW instead of dismissing gifts that aren't perfect. Rarely is anything in life perfect. That isn't a statement of disappointment. It is a statement grounded in truth. The perspective you choose can be traced back to your gratitude. *Is your glass half empty or half full?* Your answer to that question is a decision and a statement about yourself.

Before we can spread our wings and seek more of what life has to offer, let us first take a moment and inventory all the blessings in our lives. All of them! On the this page I want you to fill in the hearts as you prepare your own heart for more blessings that are coming your way.

That was a great warmup! Now I want you to take five more minutes and cram as many people, places, and things you are grateful for on this page! When I'm writing pages of gratitude I like to **turn on music** and challenge myself to write as fast as I can for the duration of one song! I want you to stretch yourself to find gratitude in the areas of your life that seem in disarray. Let your heart guide your hand and write your gratitude with an open heart.

Have fun! **Start your favorite music and write!!**

*"Gratitude is a powerful catalyst for happiness.
It's the spark that lights a fire of joy in your soul."
— Amy Collette*

Yay you! Doesn't the weight of the world feel a little lighter? Gratitude is a beautiful thing. When we are grounded in gratefulness, we have the ability to spread our wings and soar to greater heights.

When I take a few moments to write down the things I'm grateful for, it fills my heart with joy. When I'm joyful I'm much more likely to pursue my dreams and conquer my obstacles. I would venture to say you are too.

I believe success - however you define it - is a result of the relationships you forge. So be a nice person. The mountains you climb in life and the doors of opportunities that open to you will be based on a relationship 99% of the time. Yes, your peers will become the gatekeepers to the doors you are trying to open. Yes, your teachers and your boss will become your references for the jobs you are trying to secure. Don't get me wrong, your hard work and perseverance are measured on a completely different scale, but I will say those qualities of a fighting spirit may have been planted and/or harvested by a coach or a teacher or a parent or a boss. People influence our lives whether we want them to or not, and both in positive and negative ways. Choose your circle of influencers wisely. **Find gratitude for the people in your life right now!**

My mom has always taught me to give credit where credit is due. "You don't find success on your own. People help people. And when you find your success you do not want to celebrate it on your own. Invite those people who helped you to join in on the celebration." This makes me think of my hometown. Less about the actual town and more about the people. Truth be told I felt trapped by the small town I called home. The closest mall was more than a three-hour drive away while the closest international airport was a seven-hour drive. When we competed in sporting events our closest away games were at least a one-hour drive (each way), while our furthest away games were five and half hours EACH WAY! That is 11 hours on a bus and we weren't allowed to talk on our way to the competition because we were supposed to be focused – and we didn't have phones to text each other.

The most amazing things that visited our small town were the thunderstorms you could watch build over the wheat fields or the sunsets that streaked the sky with the most magnificent oranges and pinks God could paint. I loved my hometown, but at the same time I felt trapped. Trapped by little opportunity, or so I thought. I was blinded by the flat landscape and lack of tall buildings. In reality I had more opportunity than most people have in a lifetime. Because we were a small town we were expected to play every sport (because if we didn't there wasn't a team). If I wanted to participate in dance, the instructors and the coaches had to work together or they didn't have a team. My basketball coach would comment on the size and strength of my calves as he would tape my ankles before games, "it is from all the dance training," I would respond. I could tell he wanted my full commitment on the court, but in a small town he knew he had to split the time. He invested in me during the hours I spent with him, as did my dance instructor and my teachers and my neighbors, not to mention my parents and brothers and sister. Being from a small town is less about the opportunities your community has to offer (like touring Broadway shows and professional sporting events) and more about the people we serve and how we help one another thrive.

This isn't to say that community can't be found in a city. I now live in the suburbs of Denver and my neighborhood and church have turned into my small-town community. I cook for my friends when they are sick and my 80-year-old neighbor has helped me search and clear my house, weapons drawn, when I thought someone was inside (I still think there was someone in the house but they left when I went to get my neighbor).

I learned the value of relationships in my small town because that is where I was born, but I have seen that it doesn't matter if you live in a small town or a big city, there are great relationships to be developed. I believe deep down everyone wants to help one another. Invite those people along on your journey as well as in your celebrations.

When I became Miss Kansas and went on to compete at Miss America, I did not make that journey on my own. I had teams of people volunteering to help me succeed. From my track coach who taught me "pain lets you know you aren't dead yet" and to keep pushing for the championship, to my panel of 12 mock judges that grilled me for hours on everything from politics to other controversial subjects. My dance instructor gave me my own key to the dance studio to rehearse whenever I needed while my college ballet professor invited me to take classes anytime I was in town (free of charge). They were preparing me for the biggest event of my life, but in reality they were preparing me for life itself! When I made it to Miss America, one-hundred-twenty-five of my closest supporters and people who shaped my life came with me to the national competition. They were there to help me celebrate or pick me up when I didn't win. I was embarrassed when I didn't claim the title, but whether I did or didn't they were there for me. They were invested in my life.

I try to give back in the same way to the kiddos, teens, and adults in my immediate life. I want to see them succeed. More importantly I want to help.

People are good if you allow them the opportunity to be.

I love going home to my small town. Not to the town, but to the people whom I love and adore. The faces I see when I return home reminds me of how blessed I am to have such amazing people who have helped shape me into who I have become. They have helped shape my fighting spirit. Did I always like them? No. Especially my track coach on the days I was regurgitating my lunch because he was running us *that* hard. Ranch dressing is not something you want to experience in both directions. But he taught me "greatness isn't something you accidentally find; it is something you go get!" He is one of my favorite people.

I would like you to take a moment to recognize the great influencers in your life! There are many people in your life that have made a huge impact on you. As you continue to recognize your heart of gratitude, I want you to write as many of those influential people as possible who have made a positive impact in your life.

Who	**How**
Coach Cornelsen	*Expected me to perform at 100% every time I laced up my shoes. He taught me greatness isn't something you accidentally find it is something you go get!*
Mrs. Tillman	*She taught me to love reading!*
٠	

 Would you make someone else's list as a positive influencer in their life? A smart way to be a nice person is to shut up and listen. People love people who listen. Everyone wants to feel like they have been heard and understood. For more thoughts on *Who Listens To The Listener* you can access an article at www.adriennebulinski.com/guidebook

In fact, from this point forward you are going to see numerous digital resources we have waiting for you. All the upcoming resources can be accessed at the same link:

www.AdrienneBulinski.com/guidebook

Write It Down

Okay. Now that we are grounded in gratitude, let's dream!

What would you attempt to do if you could not fail? I have this quote on a refrigerator magnet and every time I reach for the door it stares at me, challenging me to answer the question.

What would you attempt to do if you could not fail?

The quote is telling me to remove the glass ceiling I place on my own life. That's right, we place glass ceilings on our own lives. Other people may try to cut us down or limit our worth, but ultimately we get to decide if there is a ceiling *or not.*

What would you attempt to do if you could not fail?

I *don't* like this quote because I know there is a fine line between success and failure. Sometimes that line is blurred because success and failure occupy the same space. Failure becomes a fear when the stakes are high. But **it is the chance of failure that makes the pursuit of success so invigorating.**

I don't want to live a life that happens *to* me. I want to pursue life and live all it has to offer. Don't you? If you are going to pursue your best life then the stakes will be high and the sting of failure will burn. You know you are pursuing something of purpose when the fear of failure is at success' heals.

What would you attempt to do if you could not fail?

What would you attempt? What is your dream? I want you to imagine your dreams in *vivid detail*. Ten years from now what are you pursuing? What does your life look like? What kind of job do you have? How many hours a day do you work? Where do you live – what kind of house/apartment/yacht do you live in or on? What city or acreage do you call your own? Who do you live with? Do you like the person/people you live with? Why? Are you a parent? What kinds of pets do you have? Where do you vacation? What do you do in your free time? Do you write books? Do you produce videos? Do you invent things to make life better? Do you like who you have become? What kind of person are you?

Start describing your life in vivid detail. Why? Because if you don't know where you're heading then how can you make a plan to get there?

Remove the glass ceiling and dream. These are your pages to write your dreams and desires. But there is a catch! **I want you to write your dreams as though they have already happened.** For example, "I am a New York Times Best Selling Author" not "I'm *going to be* a New York Times Best Selling Author." Tell your mind the truth! Do not give it a task of to-dos. Write your dreams as though they have already happened. This will feel strange, but do it anyway. Remember, the sun shines brighter outside the box.

Now write…

Dreams should be uncomfortable; otherwise they belong on your to-do list!

Move out of your comfort zone. You can only grow
if you are willing to feel awkward and uncomfortable
when you try something new. – Brain Tracey

Yes! Good for you! Look at your accomplishments and determination! Can we be friends? I need people like you in my life!

Saying your dreams out loud is the first-choice successful people make. First, it isn't easy to **say out loud** what it is that your heart is speaking to you. Why? Because this is the real you! And when you open your heart to the world you also open yourself to ridicule and other people's opinions. As my dad has told me many times "Opinions are like ass holes, everyone has one and they all stink." If you have heard me use this nugget of wisdom from the stage I have substituted the word "butt" in place of the more crude version, but in a guidebook that is about getting down to the nitty gritty I think you deserve dad's real version.

Other people's opinions of you are none of your business (a quote by Robin Sharma)! You give other people's words power… or not.

So why speak your dreams out loud?

Because you are breathing life into those dreams.

I think of dreams like seeds in a packet on a shelf. When you pick the packet off the shelf you are saying *I'm going to plant you, nurture you and grow you.* First, I'm going to stick you in the dirt and let you fight to break out of your shell. Meanwhile I'm going to dump water over your head because I know you require the struggle in order to grow. But I will keep feeding you and nourishing you because I have faith that in the proper amount of time you will pop your head up out of the dirt. With more work and nourishment you will eventually grow into a beautiful plant that nurtures butterflies or hummingbirds or bees or all three.

When I selected the seeds from the shelf I was only after the plant. Then that plant flowered. The flower provided so much more joy and benefit to the world then I was initially after. Not only did I benefit, but the creatures around me did too!

You and your dreams are no different. You will provide so much to the world! When you fully step into your purpose everyone benefits – most importantly… you! But living your purpose will not come without growing pains and that's okay.

As my track coach said over and over as we were sucking a lung, "Pain lets you know you aren't dead yet."

If you want to live your dreams you are going to have to get the dream seeds out of the packet and push them down in the dirt. Did you know most plants grow better with a little manure mixed it (be it cow or chicken)? How does this translate? Adversity makes you stronger, tougher, and more resistant to future obstacles.

"When everything seems to be going against you, remember that an airplane takes off against the wind, not with it." -Henry Ford

When you breathe life into your dreams your next choice is whether or not you nurture your dreams so they grow into what they are capable of.

But keep in mind, most packets of seeds do have an expiration date on them. In other words, there is no time like the present to plant them! The seeds and your dreams!

Do you also feel a little terrified to let yourself dream that big and in that capacity? If you don't have a nervousness in your stomach then dream bigger.

Now go bigger.

And bigger.

Yes, bigger! I know in your lifetime you have the ability to soar higher than you can imagine right now. How do I know? Look at those around you who are the the doers. Ask them what they dreamed about ten or twenty years ago and where they landed today. Ninety-nine percent of the time the doers land among wealth they had no idea how to dream of when they first started. I'm not talking monetary wealth, I'm talking about wealth in living your purpose.

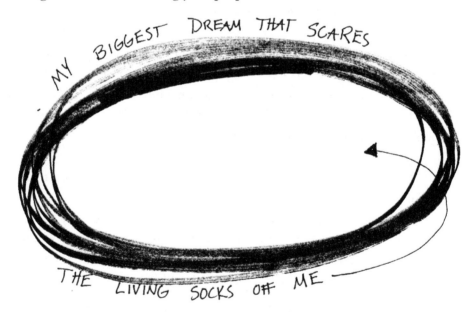

YouTube Assignment:

I want you to grab your phone and go to
www.adriennebulinski.com/guidebook
Look for the YouTube link titled "Jim Carrey"

Dirt

A message from Bill: Let's take a moment to talk about the value of **writing** something down (versus texting or typing it into a notes app). There is a tremendous power in using your hands to write your dreams. We feel the world through our hands. We even sense things through our hands: heat, cold, etc. Our hands literally open doors to our dreams.

A few years ago I had the privilege to produce a conference in Beijing, China. While I wasn't there on "vacation" we managed to see the "big" sites that Beijing had to offer; however, I also wanted to see the Great Wall of China. I will admit, it was not at the top of my list of things to do that day, but something was telling me I had to see it before I left.

You have probably seen photographs of the Great Wall (if you haven't then grab your phone and look it up). Like many things we see around the world, photographs just cannot capture the size and scope of this engineering feet. In fact, to even call it a wall is not fair. It is a massive structure going on for as far as you can see from almost any point. All built with stone. No bulldozers. No cranes. I suppose when you have almost a million people working on it for two centuries, anything is possible! It has beautiful craftsmanship and amazing masonry

21

work. The work along the Great Wall takes the thought of doing something by hand to a whole new level.

We were driven to an area that had fairly easy access to the wall and was not too overrun by tourists. We bought our tickets and made our way to the top of the wall. We walked a couple of miles along the wall as we admired the landscape. During our journey I noticed an "exit" that would take us down to the ground. As I walked along this magnificent piece of construction work, I realized something. During my nine days of being in China, I was not sure I had ever walked on anything but concrete and pavement. Something about that felt very wrong. If I hadn't actually touched the earth had I really been to China at all?

My group "decided", at my insistence, to take that exit and walk down to the ground. To stand on the dirt. Terra firma. Not stopping there, I told the three young ladies we were all going to kneel down and grab a handful of dirt. Needless to say, I received not only strange looks, but almost a revolt from them, but they followed my lead and grabbed a handful of China's finest dirt. We felt it in our hands and even went as far as smelling it. Our bodies had become one with the earth once again. No more concrete. No more cobblestones. Just us and the earth's dirt. Only then did I feel like I had connected with China.

I believe the same holds true for writing your dreams. There is a connection between your hands and your heart. So **HAND WRITE** your dreams! One of the reasons we did not make this guide an electronic piece is for that very reason. You have to think much more if you are hand writing something, be it a letter to a loved one or a dream you are finally saying out loud and committing yourself to.

Just like my connection to China required picking up a handful of dirt, your connection to your dream, along with your commitment to your dream, requires a special effort. I'm not talking about five minutes. I am talking about a much deeper vow you have made to yourself to work on your dream. By hand writing your comments in this guidebook, you will have invested that much more of yourself in the pursuit of your dream.

If you need to write more of your dreams I encourage you to do so now. Cram them onto the page. Find a space for them. You have a lifetime to pursue ALL of them!

Success

Success. What does that word actually mean? To you? So often we throw around the word "success" but we never actually stop to define it. In detail. For ourselves. The first time someone asked .... .. define success – in actual words – I was 22 years old. I almost instantly realized I had many goals and dreams I was working toward, but I had never stopped to define what success actually meant.

A few weeks after I won the Miss Kansas crown I checked into the DoubleTree Hotel in Kansas City. I was scheduled for a weekend of Miss America Competition prep with my co-executive directors. After I checked into my room and brushed some powder across my face, my directors knocked on the door to escort me to dinner. We were headed to the hotel's restaurant for a "get to know each other" dinner before we started to work. As we were casually chatting, one of them point-blank asked me "What does success mean to you?" I was so used to people asking me about my goals that I had never stopped to define what it meant to actually achieve them. I was stumped. Were they asking about success as it pertained to the Miss America Competition or success in life? The answer as it pertained to the Miss America Competition was easy... WIN.

They were asking me about success in life. I was dumbfounded I didn't have a response nor had I ever *really* thought about it. I was a recent college graduate and was proud of the accomplishment, but truth be told, a diploma was not exactly my definition of success. It was a milestone in my journey but not my destination.

What was success to me? At the age of 22? I chewed around on some ideas in my head. Within a few minutes my gut was telling me exactly what my definition of success included.

"I want a performance job I love while also being able to pay my bills."

I couldn't get through college on my own two feet financially nor could I survive my year as Miss Kansas without my parents' financial help. Success to me was being able to take care of myself. To be independent.

"How will you measure that success?" One of my directors asked. They were not only asking me to define success but how I was going to measure my progress. What kind of performance job do I want? How much money do I need to make to be independent?

I contemplated their question before I said, "To measure the dollar amount, I want to be able to buy my parents an awesome dinner at a nice restaurant in any location in the world. I want us to go all-out with appetizers, drinks, the main course and dessert. I want to pick up the tab and pay for it… WITHOUT stress."

My directors were satisfied. It wasn't the answer they were satisfied with, but the fact they had me thinking and I was able to set some mile markers to measure my progress on my journey to success.

How do you expect to know when you have "arrived" if you haven't actually defined it?

Over the next several days I challenge you to contemplate the question: **what is success to me?** There is not a right or wrong answer. It is different for everyone. But if you haven't stopped to define it then how do you know when to celebrate when you have achieved your success?

If you do not take the time to define success, I promise you that your friends and family and coworkers and a boss will be more than happy to define success for YOU. They will set your standards. But a life living up to other people's standards will leave you feeling empty and as though you have fallen flat. Only YOU can define success for YOU. So how do you define success? What does success look like? How does success feel? How will you measure your progress?

I have lived the success I wrote about a few paragraphs ago! In fact, my parent's dinner was more about the dinner cruise around New York City and the live entertainment than it was about the actual food; however, we did have all the courses! And yes, I paid for it.

As my success became my way of life, I have gone back to the drawing board and expanded my success to greater levels. It is equally important to note that because I was striving for such grand achievements, I have landed at an even greater honor of performing as a motivational speaker. Measures of success can and do change.

Defining success gives you a destination you are working toward. It is no different than planning a trip to the top of a mountain. How are you going to get to the peak? How will you prepare? What items do you need in your pack? How will you measure your success? Is success in the picture you take at the peak or is it in the round-trip journey or in the memory in your mind?

To get you started thinking about success FOR YOU I want you to fill in the bubbles (on the next page) as you would define success for YOUR life.

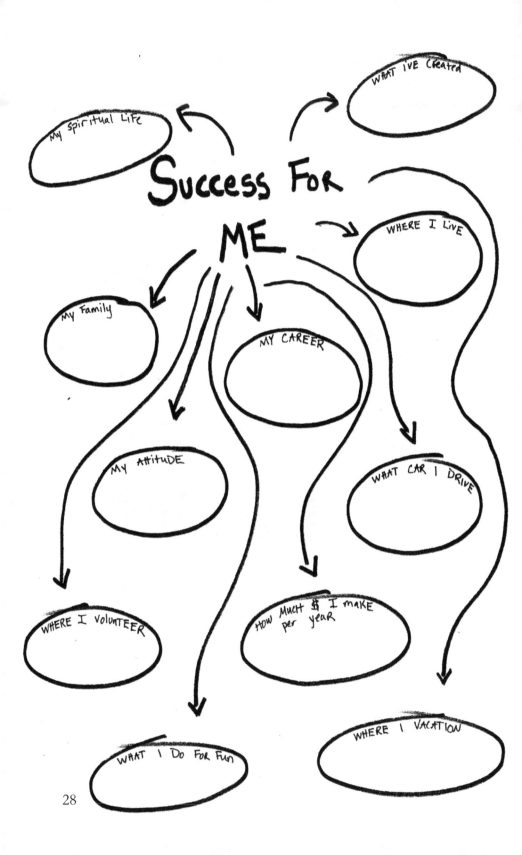

28

Over time my definition of success has grown and shifted and changed as I have. So will yours. **I have also learned that success is not always measured by dollar signs.**

It is fun to define success so you can create a plan to go get it! In fact, every so often it is important to also 1) look at your current success, regardless of the level you have achieved and 2) set new success goals.

How do you **define the difference** between

achieving goals
&
calling those achievements a success?

On this page, I want you to define success in more detail than we did in the bubbles. Get detailed. Dream! I want you to get far more detailed then I did at the age of 22. Have fun. Go!

At first they will ask why you're doing it. Later they'll ask how you did it. - Unknown

I can therefore I will. Watch me!

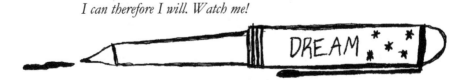

YouTube Assignment:
I want you to grab your phone and go to
www.adriennebulinski.com/guidebook
Look for the YouTube link titled "Will Smith"

Gratitude Assignment

We have been focusing on "me me me". Let's go back and gain some perspective by re-grounding ourselves in our gratitude. Remember that page where you wrote down the influential people in your life? (It's on p. 11-12). I want you to circle one of those people. Next, I want you to hand write that person a heartfelt letter grounded in your gratitude for what they have brought to your life. We even provided a page for you to do it! This means: Do not type it. Do not text it. Do not email it. Write it. With your hand!

#grateful

33

Failure

Do your dreams scare you? Just a little? FYI they should!

What if you fail? What if you can't make it happen?

I would bet my life savings you are doubting yourself in some capacity or another. You know why? Because we all do. Every successful person I have met has had to fight the good fight to overcome their self-doubt and fear of failure. Let's address this right now.

You are going to fail. In fact, I hope you experience grand failure. You want to know why? Because that means you are pushing yourself. **If you never fail, then you will never grow fully into who you were created to become.** Our greatest lessons are supported by our greatest failures. In fact, I believe we must stand on our failures to reach the success we are truly capable of reaching, but if you do not push yourself then you will never fail and therefore you will never know the success that is yours.

Let's talk about failures you have already experienced. Whether it happened to you or because of you; let's talk about.

This is scary and I get it, but I want you to see you are still breathing and still fighting and that there are many beautiful lessons in your failures that have shaped your character. **You cannot always control what happens to you, but you can control how you respond to it.**

In high school track I competed in high jump, triple jump, 300 hurdles and 100 hurdles. I'm convinced it was less about my speed and more about my height that made all my coaches think I needed to jump over things. Or perhaps it was my personality. I rarely backed down from a challenge and would rather charge an obstacle then run away from it. No matter my coaches' reasonings, I competed in the events they put me in.

I remember one race in particular. It was early in the season and the cool breeze mixed with the warm sun was energizing. I felt strong yet nervous to chase my desired first place prize. As I stood at the starting line, I shook my legs and did a few power jumps as the official said, "Runners take your marks." I took one last look at the ten hurdles spread before me with the finish line just beyond the tenth hurdle. I had one hundred meters to sprint. I had a good lane: lane three. Rarely was I in the middle – where the fastest people ran – but I wasn't in lane one or eight either so I was confident, but knew I would have to give it my all.

I leaned forward to touch my toes and stretched my hamstrings before I extended my legs back behind me to give my calves a last stretch. I continued theatrically making my way into the blocks. It should be noted: I was very good at the dramatic performance of getting *into* the blocks.

I focused on the calmness of my breath as I placed my fingers on the outside of my lane and lower my head – signaling the official I was done with my pre-performance routine: as though he was waiting on me.

"Set!"

Boom.

I exploded out of the blocks like a cheetah chasing its prey. As I cleared hurdle numbers one, two, three, and four I was in the front of the pack. I got an adrenaline rush out of charging a hurdle at full speed and skimming it so close I would kick it with my heel - causing splintered wood to fly in all directions. I gave myself an internal devilish laugh at the badass I was. I'm not sure that really justifies being a badass, but in high school it made me feel tough.

I was charging for the finish line and a medal. Then hurdle five. Hurdle six. Hurdle seven. Track.

I hit my trail leg with a hard, painful *thug* before I tumbled over myself and face planted on the track, stopping on my chin. I managed to score some impressive road rash on my landing. I could feel the sting on my skin, but worse was the sting of watching all the runners pass me by.

I didn't give it a second thought as I jumped up and charged hurdle eight then hurdle nine then hurdle ten. I crossed the finish line with as much speed as I could get my legs to produce. Dead last. By a long shot. Blood dripping. It sucked.

All my friends were watching. My parents too. As were my coaches. I felt beat up – physically *and* emotionally.

The lesson: I would have never crashed… if I never tried. When you show up for your life you will fall down from time to time, but you also have the opportunity to grow through the failure. It has been many years since that race yet it is one of my most memorable. Why? **Because I finished** (no participation trophies were issued). Although at the time I didn't feel this way, it wasn't about winning the race itself. It was about the character I was developing through my struggle.

I control *how* I finish. So do you. No, it may not always be the outcome you are looking for.

I left blood and skin on the track that day. The pain in my body and my crushed ego were some of the building blocks I would need to accept rejection when it hurt the most. It may have also been part of the life lessons that would prepare me to survive one of the biggest injuries of my life… when I severed my foot. **I may not control what happens to me, but I most definitely control how I respond to it!**

I remember that race more prominently then the first hurdle race I ever won. It was *that* race, when I face planted myself, that made me realize I really am a tough chick because I had chosen to be one. Sometimes it's the race that gets us going, but it is our attitude that determines where and how far we go.

On the next page I want you to write down your failures or major obstacles. I also want you to write the silver lining. What did you learn in that boo-boo which broke your heart or threatened to break you? On the top of the line write the challenge and on the bottom write the lesson.

Did a boyfriend or girlfriend break your heart? What qualities did he/she show you that you seek (or don't seek) in your desired life partner? Did you have an accident or tear an ACL and now you are out of your sport for a season? What lessons are you learning about your character that will help you through your next challenge? What doctor or nurse showed you compassion that you want to apply to your own life? Did you fail an exam or didn't get the SAT score you needed to apply for a particular college? What did that teach you about your study habits or how to ask for help or how to seek a better study group? Did you get fired from a job? What did it teach you about the kind of employee you are or the kind of boss you will become?

WRITE YOUR FAILURE/OBSTACLE ABOVE The Line

Write WHAT You Learned BeLow THE Line

Stuff That SUCKED!

40

My friends, the lessons are there as are the silver linings. Yes, sometimes the silver linings will feel like a stretch, but they are there. Look for them. I want you to reflect upon any failures and celebrate the fact you showed up in the first place, because if you didn't show up you wouldn't have failed. And remember that our greatest lessons, and moments in which we build our character, is the phoenix that rises out of hardships.

Do you know what a phoenix actually is? It is a mythological bird that lived for five or six centuries in the Arabian desert. At the end of its time it would burst into flame and be reborn from the ashes. This is where the famous line "rising from the ashes" comes from.

What did you learn? What has that life experience shown you? How have you grown through the challenge (even if it is the smallest amount of growth in the history of the world)? It is imperative that you see the good in the challenge. Prove to yourself you are a phoenix!

Success is not final, failure is not fatal: it is the courage to continue that counts.
-Winston Churchill

I can accept failure, everyone fails at something. But I can't accept not trying.
-Michael Jordan

Perfection is not attainable, but if we chase perfection we can catch excellence.
-Vince Lombardi

41

YouTube Assignment:
I want you to grab your phone and go to
www.adriennebulinski.com/guidebook
Look for the YouTube link titled "Sara Blakely"

You are a warrior! You are an overcomer! You have tenacity, persistence, and stubbornness to survive obstacles that have challenged your character… and you are still here. You are still dreaming and pursuing your passion and building your life. You have more strength then you give yourself credit! Seriously! How do I know this? Because you opened a guidebook that was created to help you build the life you know is yours. That is worth celebrating.

Life isn't meant to be easy. The good news: we are born with the muscles to persevere. But just like a baby is born with muscles to walk and run and play, a baby can't even lift his own head the day of his birth. It takes days, weeks and months to develop the muscles to live a full life. In fact, when that baby is learning to walk, how many times does he fall down in the process? Does he give up? No. Neither do you!

failures
are the prerequisite
and
preparation for
success
-Rebecca Rusch

The hardships you listed on the previous page are life's way of helping you strengthen your muscles of perseverance. I love Tom Hanks' quote from *A League of Their Own* "It's supposed to be hard. If it wasn't hard, everyone would do it. The hard is what makes it great."

Isn't that so true? I believe those hardships of life, where we stumble, are the very blocks of life that give us the strength to step up our game. Every time we step up our game the challenges in front of us will be bigger. However, our muscles are stronger as well.

Please don't dismiss what you have been through. Use it. Woe is not you unless you decide to live a life of woe. I have so many past experiences that I could say "woe is me...poor me..." and roll around in my hurt and shame. Instead I own it and use my stubbornness to find the good in it. I use my tenacity to find a way to use it for good so I can make a difference in this world. I want to leave this world better than I found it and I know you do too. It is going to take all of us using our individual gifts and talents to make a difference. Our world needs you and your life experiences – both good and bad.

Whether my challenges are a speed bump or a mountain, I ground myself in prayer. I believe it is our Creator that gives us the audacity to use a hardship as a blessing. Why? Because He has so much more in store for use then we have for ourselves.

When I get really stuck in the mud about something, I refer back to some very valuable Bible verses. They serve as reminders we are made for more, but it is also our hardships that shape us into the greatness we are destined to own.

Struggles produce perseverance; perseverance, character; and character, hope. (Romans 5:4)

This verse is from Romans and here is the question I ask myself when reflecting on the message: do I not want to be a person of good character that knows how to persevere? Do I not lean on hope for all things including the passions I am currently pursuing? Those beautiful qualities are all rooted in my struggles. Those qualities are the silver lining I can only find in the struggle. That struggle has the ability to blossom into a beautiful flower that becomes more than I could have wished for... and that is why I find prayer far more powerful than a wish.

So yes, I will lean into the knowledge that my struggles produce perseverance; perseverance produces character, and character produces hope.

And then I fast forward a few books and it is James that tells us **"let perseverance finish its work in you so you may be complete and lacking nothing."** (James 1:4)

My translation: I must know a struggle if I'm going to own perseverance and when I own perseverance I am complete.

Finally, I combine those two verses with the fact we are told, **"For I know the plans I have for you... plans to prosper you and give you hope."** (Jeremiah 29:11)

Life is not void of hardship, but we are reassured that the most beautiful qualities life has to offer are perseverance, character, and hope – all of which come directly from our hardships.

Today let's celebrate your scars and the strength they have given you! On the next page I want you to fill in the blanks. Celebrate YOU and the beautiful qualities of what makes you *YOU*. Channel your hardships into what it means for you to become a superhero in your own life. Every superhero I know develops their superhero skills to solve a problem or overcome an obstacle... there isn't any reason you can't do the same thing!

YouTube Assignment:
I want you to grab your phone and go to
www.adriennebulinski.com/guidebook
Look for the YouTube link titled
"Overcomer". HINT: this is a link to a song
that is a perfect soundtrack to listen to while
you write!

if you want the rainbow you gotta put up with the rain
-Dolly Parton

I AM STRONGER THAN I GIVE MYSELF CREDIT FOR!.

I KNOW THIS BECAUSE I SURVIVED_____.

It was not easy to overcome, but I did it and I am _____ for it!

Because I'm an overcomer I also learned that I am

_____,

_____,

& _____.

I will not let anyone tell me otherwise!

The next time I face a challenge I will be _____

and face it with_____.

I know that my mind is listening to how I talk to myself.
I want my mind to believe and know...

I AM _____.

I AM _____.

AND MOST IMPORTANTLY I AM_____.

If I were to describe my favorite superhero I would use strong descriptive words like

_____, _____,& _____.

Today I vow I will not_____for a superhero

BECAUSE I HAVE IT IN ME TO BE THAT SUPERHERO!

Will it be easy?_____ Will it be worth it? _____

My first heroic act is to remind myself I am

_____.

47

Pick and Go!

I will ask you again: **What would you attempt to do if you knew you could not fail?**

I want you to write down your top ten dreams in present tense.

For example…

Correct: I **_have_** produced a YouTube video that has 5 million views.

Incorrect: I'm **_going to_** produce a YouTube video that has 5 million views.

The reason you do not want to write words such as "going to" is because it signals your brain that it is another item on your to-do list. Start training your brain that your dreams are truths, not wishes.

Write ten dreams as though they have already happened.

1_____

2_____

3_____

4_____

5_____

6_____

7_____

8_____

9_____

10_____

God placed the best things in life on the other side of fear. -Will Smith

Hello massively successful person that is rocking it while making a difference in the world! Look at you and look at your dreams.

I'm so proud of you for the accomplishments you are going to see and feel in your life. I'm also proud of you for writing them down. So many people only wish their dreams would come to fruition. They hold their wishes captive in their hearts, but you have the courage to write them and now we are going to make them happen!

When I speak a dream out loud for the first time I feel a mix of overwhelming excitement which is quickly followed by deep rooted terror. How in the world am I going to make these dreams of mine come true?

The first time I announced, "I'm writing a book." My family looked at me quizzically while I smiled.

"About what?" my dad asked.

"My story. My injury. What I've learned."

My mom looked at me with concern, "Why would you open those wounds?"

"Because. I have to. I have to share my story."

I knew I could help people by being authentically raw and the best way I knew how to do it was by putting my story on paper. I wanted to write a book of triumph over tragedy. That book is now called "Blood Sweat & Tiaras" (it is on Amazon if you are curious). More important, I had a burning deep down inside that I was *supposed* to do this. But I had no idea how! The task was daunting and just thinking about it made me want to take a nap – a nap like a fat cat lying in the warm sun with no desire to actually chase something like a mouse.

I knew I had to tell someone who would hold me accountable, so I called my friend Bill Anderson. Truth be told, Bill had been trying to get me to write my story for over six years, but I wasn't ready. I knew when I announced "I'm going to write my story" there would be no turning back, at least not with him. He would (and did) hold my feet to the fire.

For the first month of writing I sincerely struggled to understand what I had decided to do. The project was so big, too big, that I quickly realized I was ill prepared to know *how to* tackle it. But I had spoken it out loud and now Bill was holding me accountable. He kept telling me "just write" so I did. I kept writing. For a year and a half I kept writing. Some of it was awesome. Some of it was a steaming pile of poop – the kind you aren't sure you will ever get the stink out of the treads of your shoes. Some of my writing made it into the book. Some did not.

Bill and I began talking as though it was complete. We knew it existed in the world and that the world needed it, we just hadn't finished the project YET. As my wordcount grew I found my rhythm. I knew "author" was a part of my resume – in present tense – so I worked to make the fact a true fact.

Now, I want *you* to go back to your top ten list and circle **the one dream** you are going to **focus** on **first**.

I'm going to show you my game plan on how I get things from a desire to an action to a truth.

Go back.

Right now.

Circle it.   BE AWESOME !!

Go do it.

Good. Now re-write that dream you are going to focus on first:

_____

Now imagine placing that dream at the top of a staircase. It isn't just any staircase though. It is a staircase of 1000 steps. While you can see your dream at the top, you can't quite make out the details. That is okay because you know it is there and now you are going to come up with a plan to march yourself up the stairs.

Overwhelming anxiety… that is how I would describe the feelings I have whenever I am standing at the bottom of a new staircase and staring up at my dream. What calms my heart is reassuring myself I only have to focus on one step at a time.

The reason I had you circle **one** dream is because you can only climb one staircase at a time.

Did you digest that? **One. Staircase. At. A. Time.**

I want you to live all of your dreams in your lifetime, but we need to focus on one dream at a time if we expect to be successful.

"You can't ride two horses with one ass." That lovely line is from the movie *Sweet Home Alabama.* Just like you can't ride two horses with one ass you can only walk up one staircase at a time.

I can also compare climbing your staircase to climbing a mountain, which might feel more appropriate when you are looking at the journey in front of you.

You can't climb more than one mountain at a time. You pick your first mountain and charge it, learn from it, build muscle, and eventually reach the top. Guess what? It may even take you a few tries to get to the top. That's right. You may not reach the top on your first attempt. You may fail. Yes, fail! Does that mean you quit? No. It means you adjust, learn, reorganize, train smarter, and you go for it again.

I live in Colorado and I love nothing more than spending time in the mountains. I love hearing the birds chirp and seeing the deer graze as I mountain bike. I love chasing butterflies down single-track trails among the wildflowers that bloom in vibrant yellows and pinks and purples. I love the sound of the breeze as it whistles through the evergreens yet sounds different among the aspens. Every trail I explore I am learning and growing and changing. I am challenging myself to become better. I am training for life, both physically and mentally. But it never fails, at least once a year we run into a lowlander (someone visiting from a state with a lower elevation). They are trying to cram a lifetime of the Rockies into a weekend vacation. But if they do not acclimate to the altitude they can get *horribly* sick. Hospital worthy sick. You do NOT show up in Colorado – from a state like Florida – and hike to the top of a 14,000 foot mountain on your first day. Just like you do not fly to Nepal and hike to the top of Mt. Everest as soon as you arrive. There is an entire acclimation period.

If you expect to show up and get to the top of a mountain on your first day (or achieve your dreams overnight) you need a reality check! Take inventory of your skills, get acclimated and train on the lower mountains before you attempt to climb the granddaddy of the daddy of mountains!

Tall mountains scare me (so do big dreams), but just like I conquer the mountain one step, or one peddle crank, at a time you too can conquer your fears and live your dreams. You climb the staircase to your dream one step at a time.

What about all your other dreams?

You can live all of them! To continue the mountain analogy: the people who climb to the top of 14,000 foot mountains rarely stop at one. It is addictive. I am addicted to mountain biking. I cannot ride one trail. I want to ride them all! But I didn't start that way. I was terrified of the rocks and the obstacles and my shaking muscles. I was nervous to trust my husband, who was my boyfriend at the time, as he held my seat post running down the mountain beside me coaching me on the obstacles. And the first time I fell... I sat on the side of the mountain and debated if it was worth it. But I was miles from the trailhead which meant I had to get back on and ride. And ride I did. Better. With more skill because I learned from my failure.

When you teach yourself to conquer your first staircase you will have the skills to tackle more staircases. I do believe the first is the hardest.

When you stand at the base of your second staircase, your survival kit is better equipped with the strength, knowledge, and lessons you learned from the first staircase. But the only way you are going to fill your survival kit is to get going. Take the first step.

On the next few pages I have a diagram I use in my own life to help me focus on the actual steps of my staircase and map out a plan.

Study the staircase and the instructions. On p. 58 and p. 59 you get to write your own plan.

Instructions on how to fill out your staircase:

1) Write that dream you circled (on p. 49) at the top of your staircase where it says "Where I'm Headed". Write it in vivid detail.

2) On the bottom step I want you to describe - with brutal honesty - where you are today. Write this on the step that says "Where I am".

3-5) What are three steps (aka: Needs) on your staircase that you must absolutely accomplish if you are going to step foot on the top step? Write the three items on your stairs next to the numbers 3, 4, and 5 where it says "Need". The steps may take months or even years to accomplish and that is perfectly okay.

6-8) What will the steps lead to? What mini-victories will you experience as you stand on each step?

9) Work on the plan EVERY DAY for at least the amount of time a piece of gum has flavor! I will explain this in more detail in the upcoming pages; however, for the time being I want you to trust me. Please note: you should be focused on one stair step at a time.

When you accomplish a step... Celebrate! Encourage yourself to find as much joy IN the journey as you anticipate at the destination!

On the following pages is your own staircase. Fill it out.

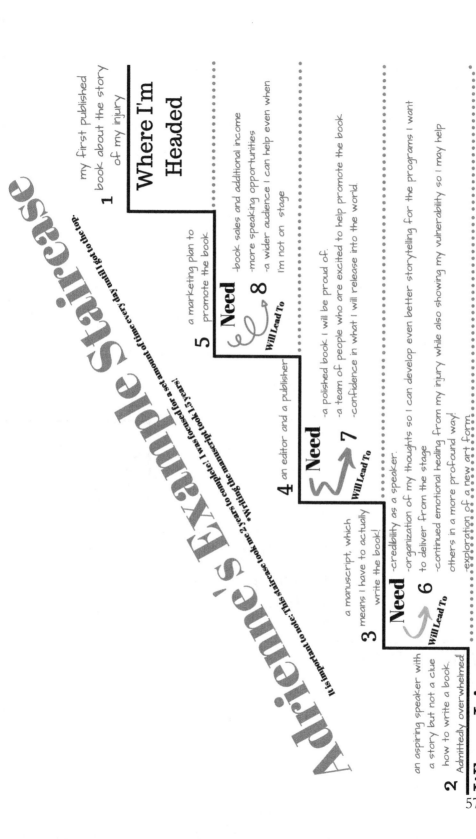

A plan is to prepare you, not to scare you!

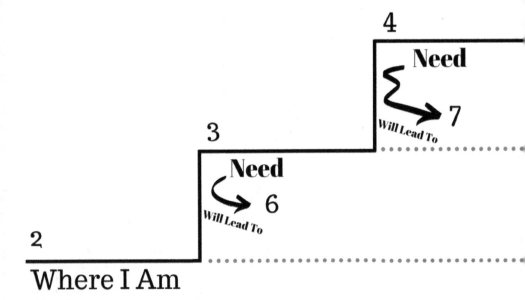

1

Where I'm Headed

5

Need

Will Lead To **8**

Download and print more staircases at www.adriennebulinski.com/guidebook

Yes, there will be a gazillion little things you must accomplish to get to the top of your grand staircase, but the three steps on your staircase are your mile markers and your focus. They are also your scheduled celebrations! Yes, you MUST celebrate along your journey. If your only celebration is planned for when you reach the top then I want you to put this guidebook down right now. This isn't for you. This is a journey, not a destination. We will always have destinations in our lives and if you cannot enjoy the journey and learn to celebrate along the way then what is the point? Besides, celebrations are rooted in gratitude. Make the commitment now that you will celebrate the small victories with as much enthusiasm as the final destination!

When I was writing my first book there were many times my staircase felt too steep. Where I started (with a blank computer screen) and where I was headed (to publication) was two years of stubbornness and determination to not only write a book, but to write a book I was proud of. I slowly started telling people I was in the process of writing my first book. I was saying it out loud. At first the words were foreign and scary, but slowly I found my routine in writing and every time someone asked how my writing was progressing it not only held me accountable, it kept me fueled. Yes, there were times I wanted to quit. I was overwhelmed by the scale of the project I had taken on (especially having no clue what I was doing). So I broke my project into three sections - writing, editing, and publishing. I knew I had to focus on one step at a time, but I also knew they would all build upon each other. The writing took me 1.5 years. The editing four months and the publishing (which included book layout, a photoshoot and cover design) two months. To make the stair step of writing manageable I broke that portion down into three sections of content and I started chipping away at the mountain. When I was feeling lost in the project that was bigger than I was I went back to my original staircase and started dreaming. At one point I even started a book-launch party guest list of all the people I would invite to help celebrate the victory. I imagined the celebration and the sense of accomplishment. My husband laughed when he figured out why I was sketching names on napkins and the back of envelopes and a brown paper Chipotle bag. "Why do I keep seeing lists of names?" he would ask.

"Because they are invited to my book release party!"

"Don't you have to finish the book first?"

"Yes, sir. I'm keeping myself fueled."

We both would laugh, but before he left the room he would add a couple of his own names to the list.

The day I finished the writing portion of my staircase was a day of **huge** celebration. I knew when I typed the last "period" the rough draft was complete. I got up from the keyboard and did a BIG happy dance for myself before I went to find my husband to jump up and down in celebration. That day even my cat knew something was going on. If you do not know much about cats - or don't even like cats - you will like this... cats bring their people presents. This particular cat, Luna, helped me write my first book  by napping behind my computer screen or she slept in the desk drawer beside me. (If you want to see a picture you can check it out on www.adriennebulinski.com/guidebook). The day I finished my book she brought me three dead mice and dropped them at my chair. She has never brought me three (not even two) on any day before or since that day.

The point is: celebrate each landmark and invite those around you to celebrate as well. You are going to need their encouragement when the going gets tough. Remember the quotes about **struggles** and **perseverance** and **character** and **hope**?

Now it is your turn to write your grand staircase if you haven't already. Yes, there may (and probably will) be staircases leading to your grand staircase, but we have to start somewhere. The keyword being **start**.

You have a staircase. Now what? Go for it! Start with the first step and zero in on it. What do you need? What skill? What accomplishment? Obviously if it is on your staircase then it is something you have *yet* to accomplish, but will in due time. I promise you have the answers within yourself to figure out how to make those stair steps become your reality. When I say you have the answers within yourself I also mean you may have to look to others for guidance and expertise, but your willingness to seek out the answers will land you in the right place.

Now with laser like focus I want you to zero in on how you are going to get there. Use your stubbornness you wrote about a few pages ago. Do NOT take "no" for an answer and go!

Now go get it!

Gratitude Assignment

Now that we have been focused on "me me me" let's reground ourselves and get some perspective. I want you to open your social media account (you choose which platform). Not active on social media? No problem. Open the contacts on your phone. Don't have a phone? Grab a piece of paper and pen. Whatever your medium, I want you to pick someone and send them a kind message. You have the ability to make someone's day a little brighter so why not do it? Not to mention, a person in pursuit of greatness *always* has the time to stop and smell the roses and appreciate those around them. Besides, kindness is contagious.

Write your dream (as though it has already happened) in the space below:

Take Five

*B**ut I don't have time....*

Buts and butts are to sit on. No excuses here. Yes you *do* have time. Let me prove it.

If you are complaining you don't have time to pursue your dream we have bigger issues and it is time to re-evaluate your priorities. This is your dream! When you know deep down in your gut this is what you are made to do… you will find a way! When your thoughts bring you back to your dream over and over again then it is time to quit denying what the universe is trying to prompt you to pursue. Remember, **the world needs you and your gifts**! No one can tell you if you can or cannot bring your dream to fruition. The only person standing between you and your dream is you!

This is your dream and WE need you to live your best life! Do you hear that? WE NEED YOU! The world needs YOU and the awesomeness you have to offer.

Now that you are standing at the bottom of your staircase, how do we do this?

I have found that five minutes is all the springboard you need to launch into your version of awesome.

Let me explain.

The pursuit of a dream can feel like a daunting task. I used to argue with myself that I didn't have time in my day to find another hour. However, as a ten-year-old I discovered a powerful lesson: the power of five minutes.

One day when I walked into my fourth-grade classroom, Mrs. Tillman told the class we were going to work on a project. She was going to ask each one of us what we wanted to be when we grew up. She was going to write it down and save that piece of paper. She then went on to explain she would be at our high school graduation (which was very believable when you live in a small town) and she was going to hand us the piece of paper and ask us one question, "What have you done to make your dream become a reality?" Immediately I had mixed feelings of excitement as well as fear. Excitement because I knew what my dream was and this teacher was taking it serious. The fear was because I had no idea how I was going to make it happen and she was going to hold me accountable! As a ten-year-old I loved the challenge.

As she started around the classroom, my anxiety grew as I heard Josh say he wanted to be a professional baseball player, Nikia wanted to be an author, Luke wanted to be a pilot, and so on.

"Adrienne, what do you want to be when you grow up?"

"A professional dancer!" I said with unashamed enthusiasm.

That evening I took inventory of the skills I needed to become the dancer I had so boldly and proudly proclaimed. I had visions of grand theatres with red fabric seats and multiple blinding spotlights. I could feel the coolness of a large auditorium along with the sounds of sporadic sniffling and the shuffling of playbills. Yes, I could feel and imagine where I was headed in life!

I immediately knew one of the skills I needed to acquire if I ever expected to be that dancer on grand stages was *the splits*. Dancers have the ability to kick their legs effortlessly (imagine a Rockette kick-line) as well as leap across the stage doing the splits in midair (imagine a ballerina as she gracefully leaps from one side of the stage to the other). The problem: I had zero flexibility. But that wasn't going to stop me.

After dinner I went up to my room and flipped over an hour glass I had on my dresser. I used the hour glass as a timer while I stretched. I made myself focus until the sand fell from the top of the hour glass to the bottom - exactly five minutes.

Every night after dinner I followed this same routine. It wasn't until three years later I could sufficiently do the splits – without crying in pain.

THREE YEARS!

I learned a valuable lesson. Five minutes. All it takes is five minutes a day to form a routine. And that routine can deliver results!

But it took you so long! THREE YEARS!

So what! It taught me the journey is in your focus **every day**. If I would not have made the challenge **so simple** I would have tried a few times and then quit.

Keep. It. Simple. Stupid!

That is one of my favorite sayings. Keep it simple stupid. **Keep it simple so you actually do it**. Five minutes was simple for me so I did it. So can you!

The mind is powerful and I believe there is more muscle in the mind than the physical body. Train your mind to crave the time to focus EVERY DAY. You will chip away at your mountain and you will get to the top.

Or as one of my friends likes to say, "You eat an elephant one bite at a time." Thank you Jerry H. for this great, yet visually disgusting nugget of wisdom!

As I got into middle school and high school I used the five minute challenge to develop a six pack on my stomach. What would your stomach look like if you spent five minutes a day doing crunches? Earlier I would bet you were skeptical about there being power in five minutes. Oh my friend, five minutes is the launch point. Need another example? A couple of years ago I wanted to develop the muscles in my

arms, but I couldn't even do a push up. I started with five push-ups from the knees. It was embarrassingly hard! I did that every morning for almost two weeks. As time progressed it got easier so I increased my reps. I increased the challenge by increments of five until I was doing 25 pushups from the knees *easily*. Once I could do 25 from the knees, I reduced my pushups back to five full plank military push-ups. Yes, it was hard! However, by the time I was two months into my challenge I was doing sets of 10 full plank military push-ups every morning. At three months

I was doing sets of 25 – pretty easily I might add. The added bonus: my stomach muscles were tightening as well. And never in my push-up challenge did I spend more than five minutes focused on my goal.

I like small physical challenges to prove a theory works.

I wrote this workbook and my first book using the same method. Considering it was a bigger project and larger dream than merely the splits, a six pack, or buff arms I realized I needed to reevaluate my approach. I was NOT going to write a whole book in one sitting or one month. So I broke it down. I challenged myself to turn off the Internet, turn off my phone and open a word document. I had to sit in front of that word document for at least thirty minutes a day. I could sit and do nothing or I could sit and write. There were multiple days I couldn't find my groove and as I pecked at the keyboard I would start fighting with my mind that I was wasting time. But **I said I was going to do something and so I was holding myself accountable.** Sometimes it wasn't until minute marker 29 that I would find my flow and more times than not that writing session was at least an hour if not two. That is the beauty in the challenge of doing something every day… even if for only five minutes.

When you say you are going to do something, do it! Even if it is only five minutes!

If I asked you, "Could you accomplish something great (as it pertains to your dream) if I showed you how to find 1,825 minutes to focus on it?" Every person whom I have ever asked this question has said unarguably "Yes!"

Five minutes a day times one year equals 1,825 minutes!

Here is the math:

5 minutes x 365 days = 1,825 minutes

68

Let me put this in sports terminology. Let's say you need to enhance your basketball game. Your free throw percentage is less than 80%. What if you spent five minutes a day – outside of practice, outside of commitments, etc – to shoot free throws? In those five minutes do you think you can shoot at least ten free throws? Absolutely!

Here is the math:

5 minutes = 10 free throws x 365 (one year) = 3,650 free throws.

If you shoot 3,650 free throws **more** than expected what do you think is going to happen?

I'll leave the free throw analogy at that.

But – yes I know buts and butts are to sit on – but, I wanted something a little more dynamic to prove my point regarding the five minute challenge. I was on the hunt for an idea.

----- ----- -----

The year was 2005 and I had recently been crowned Miss Kansas. As state titleholders (be it Miss Kansas, Miss Texas, Miss New York or any of the other state representatives) we immediately had a microphone thrust into our hands, so we better have something worthwhile to say. State titleholders are invited to speak at events, at schools, to sponsors, you name it. What we choose to share during our year is very much a part of the interview process as we compete for the title. What we choose to highlight is called a *platform*. What is a cause that we want to shed light on? Every girl chooses something that is important to her. My platform was two-fold: 1) I wanted to help people strive for their life's calling (sort of what I do now) as well as 2) have the financial education to make it happen. In 2005, I saw a major shortcoming in our education system and the oversight of neglecting to teach teens how to survive in the world financially.

I got to work.

I lobbied my state legislatures and started speaking out on the lack of financial education in schools. I was catching some attention, which included the attention of Koch Industries headquartered in Wichita, KS. Koch Industries is the second largest privately held company in the country and the founder, Charles Koch, is estimated to have a net worth of $50.8 billion! That is billion with a B. While the Koch empire began in the oil industry it has expanded to include a plethora of businesses that are dedicated to improving our lives and our world. Since this isn't a guidebook on the innerworkings of Koch Industries I will leave the rest of their history up to your research (if you so choose). The point is: I caught the attention of Koch Industries in 2005 when I emerged as a "beauty queen" talking about the importance of a solid financial education.

Charles, and his wife Liz, had formed an organization I had never heard of, but was about to quickly jump in and be a part of. These two billionaires saw a lack of entrepreneurial education, which included a financial education, in the local high schools (in and around Wichita) so they decided to do something about it. Enter *Youth Entrepreneurs of Kansas*. This organization pairs local businessmen and businesswomen with local high schools. The adults go to the schools to teach business education and entrepreneurship to teens. The teens are guided through a program where they get to bring their own business ideas to life. At the conclusion of the program they get to present their business plans to a panel of judges. At least this is how it worked in 2005 when I sat on the same panel, as a judge, with Liz Koch. When I first met her I was

70

starstruck by the massive diamond studs that decorated each ear. Diamonds aside she was warm, friendly, and gracious.

As the rules of the presentations were being explained to us (the panel of judges) I raised my hand to ask, "What do they win?" I don't remember all the details except the winning boy and the winning girl would also be going on an all-expense paid trip to New York City where they would be staying at the Waldorf, meeting the CEO of Citigroup, walking the floor of the Stock Exchange, attending a Broadway show, attending a Yankee's game, and oh yes... a camera crew would be following them as they were planning to produce a promo video for *Youth Entrepreneurs*. My response to this amazing grand prize, "Do you need any more chaperones?"

Everyone laughed as we took our seats at the table and waited for the competition to begin.

As one after another budding entrepreneur presented their ideas, there was one young man in particular that caught my attention. His name was Ricardo. During his presentation he presented a giant, colorful wad of gum. It was the size of a softball. He was demonstrating how savings works. If you invest in your savings a little bit every day you are going to have great returns on your investment.

He sparked my interest! I loved the disgusting example as did everyone in the room.

When Ricardo finished his presentation he exited the room until everyone was brought back and we announced the male and female winners. Ricardo was the male winner.

I walked up to him and shook his hand and told him how impressed I was, especially with the wad of gum. I then asked him if I could use the idea.

"What do you mean?" he asked.

"I would like to run an experiment by working on my dream everyday for the duration a piece of gum has flavor. When the flavor runs out I can be done with my focus for that day. I want to see how far I get in a year – both with the size of the wad of gum and with advancing my efforts."

He loved the idea! In fact, he gave me full permission to run with it.

I did just that. From that day forward I worked on my dream every day for at least the amount of time a piece of gum had flavor (at least five minutes). I saved every piece of gum I chewed that year by sticking it to a plate. The plate traveled on the passenger seat of the Miss Kansas mobile. After 365 days I had quite the wad, but more importantly I had made great strides in moving toward my dream. For example, one of my greatest fears in life was singing in public. But if I wanted to be a performer on Broadway I had to get over that. One of my tasks was to sing anywhere and everywhere I could find the opportunity. So I did. And a lot of times I had a piece of gum tucked under my tongue.

Singing is now one of my greatest joys and I love to share my voice whenever the opportunity presents.

So what would you work on if *you* took **The Gum Challenge**? If you had to focus on your dream everyday, for at least the amount of time a piece of gum has flavor, where would it take you? What fears would you conquer? What barriers would you break? How would you improve?

There is only one way to find out. Do it! In fact, start your own wad of gum and see where it lands you. Join the rest of us who are currently participating in **#TheGumChallenge.**

By the way, at the conclusion of the *Youth Entrepreneurs of Kansas* presentations the people in charge came up to me and said, "As a matter of fact we do need another chaperone. Are you really interested? We will pay for everything."

Somewhere out in cyberspace there is a promo video for *Youth Entrepreneurs* that features Miss Kansas 2005. If you would like to see a picture of our group on the floor of the New York Stock exchange you can check it out at www.adriennebulinski.com/guidebook.

Also, the vision for *Youth Entrepreneurs of Kansas* is no longer just in Kansas therefore their name is simply *Youth Entrepreneurs* (YE). If you are interested in learning more about YE or Koch Industries you can check out their companies at ww.youthentrepreneurs.org and www.kochind.com

To achieve your goals you must apply discipline and consistency. - Denzel Washington

Reflecting back on your staircase (that you filled out on p. 58-59) I want you to rewrite what is on your **first step** (next to #3) **of your staircase** in the space below:

Now write three truths that must happen in order for you to achieve what you just wrote above.

Truth #1_____

Truth #2_____

Truth #3_____

Now I want you to circle one of those truths you will focus on first. In the space below I want you to write a plan on **when** and **how** you are going to spend at least five minutes – starting today – to own that truth and make it happen!

When:

How:

Equally as important as having a plan, how will you measure your progress? Write your ideas in the space below. For example, if you can't do ten full pushups you can measure your progress by the amount of reps you build up to.

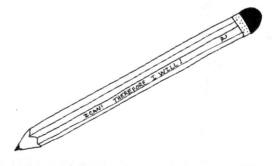

Write your dream (as though it has already happened) in the space below:

Gratitude Assignment

Remember the gratitude assignment where we had you write an actual handwritten letter? Now you get to mail it. *What?!* That's right! Mail it. As is! Go back to p. 33 and tear it out, fold it up, and place it in envelope!

Hand write the address on the envelope. Buy a real stamp and put the stamp on the envelop.

Yes, you need to mail it! In today's world, finding someone's address is possible. I find social media to be the fastest way to find someone or someone connected to that someone. Send them a private message and let them know you have a letter you would like to **mail** and you are searching for an address.

Here is how to address an envelope:

Your Name
Your Address
City, State ZIP

STAMP

SANTA CLAUS
2468 Reindeer Way
North Pole, AK 12345

Write your dream (as though it has already happened) in the space below:

Dreamer Beware

Remember, just because it is legal or you get away with it,
doesn't mean it will not destroy your dream.

One of the items that helped me on my journey – particularly when I was a teenager into my twenties – was being aware of potential land mines. What are some choices you know you will be faced with that could derail or massively set back the pursuit of your dream? The easiest three land mines I could always think of was drugs, sex and alcohol. Let me explain…

I was madly in love with my high school sweetheart. He was kind, motivated, and good looking. Not to mention I enjoyed locking lips any time the opportunity presented itself. I was crazy about him and our hormones were making *us* crazy – figuratively and literally. Why do I mention this? Because 1) it is normal and 2) it could have potentially caused a major pitfall in my pursuit of the stage. Remember, my dream was to be a dancer? If I would have gotten pregnant in high school my life's story would be massively different. Would the stage have been possible? Perhaps, but it would have been a whole lot more difficult. Because I was aware of this it was always in the back of my mind. It kept me in check as we started to get a little too hot and heavy for each other. **I had decided my actions BEFORE I was in the moment.**

I planned on marrying this guy, so what gives? As we both began zeroing in on our dreams we were both working hard. One summer evening we were hanging out at the park - playing a game of cards. We didn't have money to bet so we were betting hypothetical life experiences such as places we would vacation or cars we would buy. I remember betting a trip to "New York City". He said "no". Just like that... No. I was so confused. Why? It was just a game. He told me he had no desire to ever visit such a city. You guys, that was my dream! New York City! Broadway! And he wouldn't even hypothetically bet a trip to take me there. I was crushed. I could feel the choice before me: one of us would have to choose our dream and the other would have to push their life's purpose to the curb. It was in that moment our relationship (for me) ended. After three years. But I knew I couldn't deny my heart. At that point in my life I knew I had to follow my calling and he was telling me "no". My heart broke, but when you know, you know.

The point is: I want you to think about the potential pitfalls and setbacks you will face. How are you going to react in the situation? Do you want to play college ball? How are you going to respond when you are invited to partake in underage drinking? So you sing. What about vaping? What about drugs in general? I have been offered drugs so many times in my life I don't even want to recount it. As an adult, just because you are of a legal age doesn't mean drinking or doing drugs is a good idea. **If I didn't have a goal in front of me then I don't know what my answer would have been when presented with the opportunity to ingest legal (and illegal) drugs.**

Do your best to think through a few situations that you *know* you will face and write them below. I also want you to write your response to how you will handle those situations. **This process isn't to scare you, it is to prepare you.**

By failing to prepare, you are preparing to fail. -Benjamin Franklin

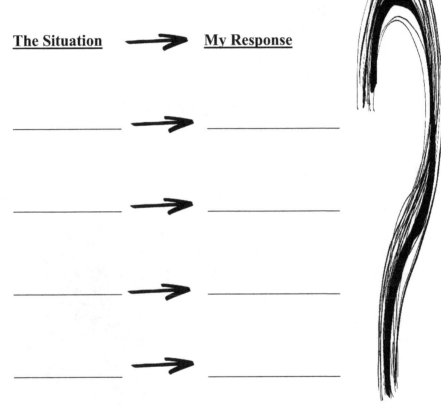

The Situation ➡ **My Response**

_____ ➡ _____

_____ ➡ _____

_____ ➡ _____

_____ ➡ _____

Some examples: (preferably when you are 21) who is going to be the designated driver when you go out with your friends? How are you going to respond when that person doesn't hold up their end of the bargain?

Write your dream (as though it has already happened) in the space below:

Anxiety

I have talked about my dream and my pursuit, but there are times I still get overwhelming anxiety. I can go from feeling like I can conquer the world to being so overwhelmed all I want to do is take a nap. My symptoms range from a racing heart to talking so fast I don't finish a word before I start the next to crying.

When I know I need to get myself in check. What is my number one go to? Exercise.

Exercise has proven, for me, to be my number one ally. If I need to get myself focused versus rattling around inside my body like a pinball machine, I exercise. If I need to generate some creative ideas, I exercise. If I need to

get myself motivated because the pursuit of my dream feels daunting, I exercise.

When I feel good about my body my mind tends to follow. If I feel good in my mind my body wants to move.

To take it a step further, I am always in pursuit of good quality food. Yes, I like Oreos and ice cream and chips (I am human after all), but I am more focused on the veggies and organic meats I put in my body. I love spinach and broccoli and garlic and pretty much anything you can pluck out of the ground! I didn't always like healthy food until I realized what it did for me and how it made me feel. I need good fuel to be a performer. I need good fuel to write good books. I need good fuel to exercise at the level I do. In fact, I need premium fuel.

What you put in your body is what you get out.

At our house we have taken this a step further. It is not just about food and exercise. What kind of things do you watch on TV or YouTube? What kind of music do you listen to? What do you read? How do you spend your downtime? What are your hobbies?

What you put in your body is what you get out.

Several years ago, when I was dreaming about becoming a fulltime speaker, meanwhile working a demanding job, I noticed my attitude was slipping. I was spending 1.5 hours a day in my car commuting. The radio stations I was tuning into were always making fun of someone or people were calling in to complain about traffic, their life, you name it. The radio commentators always had upbeat voices, but the content was not aligning with my pursuit for greater things. After a few years I started flipping the stations. I landed on a station that's tagline was "positive encouraging K-Love". I started listening. I'm still listening years later. Everything they talk about is truly positive and encouraging. The music isn't about getting drunk or going out on a Friday night. It is Christian pop radio and it hits the mark for me. It helps fuel me in my pursuit of a positive attitude and living my purpose. This was such a small change I made but the results have been tenfold! If you want to check it out, it is a nationwide station.

I invite you take inventory of your life. Where can you clean up a few areas? What are you putting in your body that isn't the best fertilizer for your dreams? **Over the next week I encourage you to keep your routine the same but take inventory.** What are you eating? What are you watching? What are you reading? What are you listening to? How are you exercising? Who do you hang out with? What do you talk about? How are you engaging on social media? How much time do you spend on social media? How much time do you spend outside? How much time do you spend away from technology? How are you actively growing your dream?

At the end of the week decide to make ONE change. You may find you already have a life of healthy living… then keep on keeping on! However, if you find your life is a train wreck, no problem. Good for you for recognizing it! Pick ONE ITEM you want to redirect and then redirect it. JUST ONE ITEM.

My high school track coach always said it takes two weeks to get in shape. I've heard other people say it takes a month to create a habit. Let's split the difference. For three weeks I encourage you to correct a negative habit and turn it into something that is a

put your phone down
and

Go Outside

fountain of encouragement in your life. It will be hard. It is always hard to get in shape, but the rewards are always worth it.

Every spring I hop back on my mountain bike and force myself to ride courses that are tough. While I am bent over the handlebars dry-heaving I envision how fun the summer is going to be! As mountain bikers we aim to get in shape as quickly as possible. Why? Because once you are in shape you get to ride long distances that are a freaking blast! My husband and I ride during the week to stay in shape, but come the weekend we are on our bikes for no less than 2.5 hours at a time. A great day with a great ride is four hours on the trail! Want to know one of my dreams as a mountain biker? There is a cabin to cabin trail from Telluride, CO to Moab, UT. It is approximately 215 miles and takes seven days to ride. That is an average of 30 miles a day traversing mountains. I can't wait! But to enjoy my time on a bike I have to eat right and fuel my body with positivity. Biking helps me get my anxiety in check and is also the place I do my best thinking and dreaming. It all works together – the dream, the exercise, the diet, the intellect.

Start cleaning up the areas of your life YOU KNOW need some work. It will be tough at the beginning but once you get in shape it makes everything flow more smoothly.

Just like you can only climb one staircase at a time I encourage you to pick only one item to address at a time. Master that one item and then move on to the next. If you try to fix everything all at once you will either suffer from burnout or you will fall flat or both. One staircase at a time my friend. And enjoy the journey. You are building muscle to live your dream.

Side note: if you have tried everything in your power to get your anxiety in check, but nothing seems to be working, it is time to start talking. Run a google search for a counselor in your area. Speak to your doctor. When I offer these suggestions I do not offer them lightly as I personally know the struggle with anxiety and its friend depression. After my injury I had to seek counsel and medication in order to be able to function. For those of you whom I am meeting for the first time through this guidebook I encourage you to read my first book. As a professional entertainer my career took a sharp detour when I was thrown from a horse and severed my right foot. The book is the journey into and out of that moment in time. A lot of what I write about when it comes to attitude, character, and perseverance was developed during that time of my life. Yes, I hit rock bottom and then sunk lower... and lower. I did not manage any of my recovery – physically or emotionally – on my own. I was surrounded by a support system. Some of those people were built in, some I had to seek. The point is, if you are suffering from anxiety and/or depression DO NOT let it rob you of your life. You WILL feel like a biology experiment as people do their best to help you. Accept your hardship and search for answers. You too will have the opportunity to use ANY hardship you experience as a powerfully positive force **if you so choose**. The very moment in time that derailed me from my goals ended up being a blessing. Was that on accident? No. I have fought to make it a positive in my life. You can too.

Treatments and choices I have used to help with my anxiety and depression:

Exercise: again, this is my number one go-to! Exercise is powerful. And ladies, if you are cramping around that time of the month then go exercise! I know you do not want to but do it anyway. The benefits are worth it. In fact, when I'm having severe cramping I get on my bike. Within 20-30 minutes the movement helps alleviate the pain.

Acupuncture: I love acupuncture! I have used it for a variety of ailments, and it seems to have a positive affect 80% of the time. When it came to battling depression a good acupuncture treatment would give me a boost for 3-5 days, but then I would revert back. For me it didn't provide a long term fix; however, I still believe this is a positive healthy alternative to try before medication.

Massage Therapy: I love a good massage! In fact, hold on as I want to book an appointment right now............. Done. As a dancer, I started getting massages in college. Taking care of my body was extremely important if it was going to last. I quickly started discovering the emotional healing that accompanied my massage treatments. Lying on a massage table for at least an hour with soothing music and the touch of another human being as they help release tension is a beautiful thing. Moreover, through all of my surgeries, massage therapy helped loosen muscle and fascia that was tightened due to severe trauma. I highly recommend massage therapy!

Vitamins and supplements: Yes, I take both. That being said, I will not advise you on vitamins and supplements as I am not a doctor. I will say my vitamins and supplements are a HUGE part of my daily routine and healthy living. They have made a profound impact on my digestive system, ability to focus, relief of muscle tension and a source of energy. They have also helped reduce any PMS that comes with being a female. I have worked with a homeopathic doctor for years. There are doctors that believe in more natural alternatives rather than chemical drugs. They are hard to come by, but they are out there if you are willing to look.

Diet: What you put in your body is what you get out. Am I repeating myself?

Use Your Calendar: Ladies listen up! Gentleman, you may skip this paragraph. Ladies, use a calendar to track your cycle! Take note of your mood swings over a few months. When do you become irritated with everyone and everything? If you want to save yourself from some massive fights with your loved ones, then be aware of the hormones that are fluctuating inside your body. Men are very confused and perplexed when it comes to women and our ability to multitask, be beautiful creatures they are desperately attracted to, and yet be terrified they may breathe wrong at least once every 30ish days. I actually feel sorry for men on occasion, my husband included, as women are beautifully complex, and men are simple. Don't worry, my husband laughs with me and agrees. The point is: I literally mark my Google calendar so it will send me a text AND email when I anticipate the approach of that hormone swing. I have discovered it is like clockwork (within a few days each month) so I forewarn my husband. He says "thank you" (no other words are exchanged) and he does a better job of helping keep the house picked up for the next few days. For me, a dirty house sets off my internal dialogue that then spirals out of control. Eventually it spews out of my mouth and it is time for a showcase of World War III. Enough about this subject… you get the point.

Antidepressant: Yes, I take an antidepressant. I am so grateful for the medication as it helps me tremendously. While I'm a little scared to publish this, I want to be completely transparent so I may help you live your best life. I recently spent ten months weaning myself from the medication. It was a very rough ten months. My cognitive mind was not engaging, I felt like I had a sweater on my tongue which made it difficult to speak. I was lethargic and I would have massive crying spells. In reality I truly felt like I was detoxing from a drug. Once I got it out of my system I started sinking into a hole. No matter how hard I tried I couldn't get my mind over matter. Yes, I had days it was hard to get out of bed (and so I didn't). I wanted my life back. With weeks of discussion with my husband, we made the decision together that it was best for me to be back on the medication. Today I am. And I'm thriving. I want you to thrive too! I still pair exercise, massage therapy, diet and all of the above with my daily dose of antidepressant. It took me ten months to discover I had a deficiency in an area of my body that involved my mind, so we fixed it.

Counseling: I firmly believe EVERYONE needs someone to talk to. We all need an outlet. Your best friend did not sign up to be your counselor. I understand talking to friends, but if you are working through some crap in your life please don't dump that on your friends. Everyone is fighting a tough battle. Seek out a counselor who is educated on how to help you. Whenever I offer this suggestion, I always get someone who says, "I don't have the money." I used to say that too. It is an excuse! Every church I have ever walked into has a pastor who will counsel with you FOR FREE! Did you get that: **FOR FREE!** The counselor that helped me THE MOST when I was recovering from my trauma was the pastor of my new church. And guess what... he counseled me FOR FREE. He is one of my best friends to this day!

Music Therapy: This is my new favorite resource! In fact, I wrote this entire guidebook listening to bilateral music. *What is it?* I'm glad you asked!

I was first introduced to bilateral music during a counseling session when we tried several rounds of brain mapping (also an interesting treatment to research). My counselor had me put on a pair of earbuds and listen to the music while she took me through some conversations (aka: therapy). I found some healing and answers using the brain mapping technique. I also enjoyed the music, so I started listening to it at home when I was writing. It helps me get laser focused while it also calms my senses.

Bilateral music must be listened to with earbuds because the music gently rotates back and forth from ear to ear. The movement is soothing. There is something scientific taking place as the music rotates back and forth - crossing your brain's midline. I don't fully understand it, but I love it. Since this isn't a research book on bilateral music I'm not going to go into the details other than it works for me, it is non-invasive and it is FREE. Why not give it a try? I have provided some links for you to get started with your bilateral music on my resource page which you can access at www.adriennebulinski.com/guidebook

 **YouTube Assignment:**
I want you to grab your phone and go to www.adriennebulinski.com/guidebook
Look for the YouTube link titled "Matthew McConaughey"

Write your dream (as though it has already happened) in the space below:

Gratitude Assignment
for the ladies

I was at a conference a few years ago and the lovely speaker Ellie Lofaro made such an interesting suggestion, "Ladies, how often are you out in the community and someone compliments you on a piece of your jewelry? 'I like your bracelet. I like your necklace.' What if we removed that piece of jewelry and handed it to them? Do we not have more jewelry than we know what to do with? Jewelry we have collected over the years and rarely wear? I'm talking about the jewelry we pick up at Target or Walmart. What if we started giving it to a sister with no expectations of receiving something in return? I encourage you to give it a try and see what it does to your heart."

At the end of Ellie's program every attendee received a handmade faux pearl bracelet with a cross on it. We all put them on. Later that day I witnessed my mom have an interaction with a hostess at a restaurant. The hostess commented on my mom's bracelet and my mom took it off and handed it to her. Words cannot describe her face and the joy she expressed. Joy from being appreciated and noticed.

It wasn't until a few years later when I was at Walmart that a woman commented on a necklace I had on. It was an inexpensive, but fun necklace I hadn't worn in several years (the last time I wore it was when I made my first speaking demo video – it was pink feathers on a gold

88

chain). The woman made a comment about my necklace and I thanked her and continued my shopping. Ellie came to my mind about three minutes later and I realized I was about to miss my opportunity… I walked back over to the woman and asked if she would like my necklace. She looked at my very quizzically, "Why?"

"Because you like it and I want to give it to you as a gift." I took it off my neck and placed it around hers.

She smiled from ear to ear and gave me a huge hug.

I don't remember anything else about that day or what I bought. All that mattered was the expression on that woman's face, not to mention the feeling in my own heart.

The lesson: **We get to be the difference makers.** In our pursuit of our dreams let us not forget that we have the power to positively influence others with our actions and our hearts of gratitude.

Write your dream (as though it has already happened) in the space below:

Attitude

Ultimately your attitude will make or break you. Period. A positive attitude is imperative. I promise, people do not rise to the top when they are weighed down by a negative attitude.

I have been scuba diving a handful of times in the waters just off the shores of Cozumel, Mexico. Because of my ankle I get to sit on the edge of the boat as my divemaster attaches weights to my belt and secures the tank on my back. As I spit into my goggles, mix the saliva around the lens and then dip the mask into the ocean water before I place it over my eyes, I am nervous to get in the great big ginormously huge body of water! My heart is always racing as I hold my goggles in place and lean forward to plunge into the cool salty water. Since I need help getting situated with all my gear, I am the first one in the water and have to wait while everyone else gets their gear on and joins me. I'm *always* on the verge of freaking out as I remind myself "yoga breaths". I'm nervous 1) because shark attacks typically happen at the surface and 2) I have so much weight strapped to me that if my vest isn't filled with the proper amount of air I will sink to the bottom of the ocean. Not only will I sink, but no one is in the water to help me AND if I go down too fast I will experience nitrogen narcosis. I have a fear of my ears bleeding from descending too fast. Silly, I know. Or is it?

So why do I scuba? It. Is. AMAZING! I have swam alongside sea turtles as well as marveled at lobsters that have been at least two feet long. I have admired sting rays as they skirt along the ocean floor only to disappear into the sand. I have entered Nemo and Dori's world of tropical fish and fierce eels. I have marveled at living coral and watched as my husband snapped his fingers and they suck themselves back inside the rock. The mystery of the ocean is both scary and deeply intriguing with its mystical beauty. As I swim along I think of my childhood and all the times I watched "The Little Mermaid" meanwhile I hum to myself "Under The Sea" and giggle into my regulator. I take deep yoga breaths as I find myself grateful I get to live in a different world for the next hour.

What does this have to do with attitude? Some things are scary when we dive off the end of the boat, but the reward in the water underneath would still be a mystery if we did not have the courage to jump in. Sometimes you have to dive in. Head first. Have faith.

Jumping in to pursue your dream is scary, but if you never jump then the reward of living your dream will remain a mystery.

But what about the weight around my waist? If I only had weight on my waist and no tank, I would sink to the bottom like a cat in a sack with rocks. If you jump into the waters of your dream with the attitude you are going to sink and die, then you will probably sink and die.

If you jump into the water and the only item that fuels you is the negative weight of the world, then you are going to sink and die. I know so many people who are in pursuit of something greater but are frustrated they never get there. The only thing I ever hear coming out of their mouths is about how our world is falling apart or they don't have enough money or life hasn't been fair to them. If you only have the weight of the world strapped around your waist you will sink and die. Put on your air tank! Fill it with positivity. You DO NOT jump in the ocean without checking, double checking, and triple checking the oxygen level on your tank. You DO NOT jump into your dream without checking, double checking and triple checking your attitude for the journey! Your secret weapon: ATTITUDE. It will determine your success!

I love what Thomas Edison had to say about inventing the light bulb, "I have not failed. I have just found 10,000 ways that won't work."

How in the world was he so positive?

What about JK Rowling and how many times her Harry Potter manuscript was rejected. Don't know the story? Look it up!

I could say the same for all these people who faced massive amounts of rejection but kept going.
- Walt Disney
- Steve Jobs
- Bill Gates
- Harrison Ford
- Stephen King
- Steven Spielberg
- Oprah
- Jim Carrey
- Vera Wang

If you want a lesson in inspiration then run a Google search or read a biography on any of the people above and how they got started! They did not experience success straight out of the gate. They had to overcome obstacles and adversity. Your fuel for resilience and perseverance is your attitude.

Need an idea on how to develop a positive attitude? It's easy… make the declaration while looking yourself in the mirror, **"I'm going to have a great day!"** This may sound cheesy, but I dare you to **try it for one month.** For one month, every morning, while you are brushing your teeth, I challenge you to make the declaration with a foamy mouth of toothpaste, "I'm going to have a great day!"

Get the declaration in your mind by writing it below. Rewrite "I'm going to have a great day":

Now write it again:

YouTube Assignment:
I want you to grab your phone and go to www.adriennebulinski.com/guidebook
Look for the YouTube link titled "US Navy Admiral, William H. McRaven"

Write your dream (as though it has already happened) in the space below:

Do you realize I have asked you nine times to write your dream? That's not an accident. It is to get you in the habit of keeping your dream in front of you during your pursuit so you don't lose your focus.

GO!

My friend, **GO!** Go pursue your dreams! You have all the tools you need to make your dream become your reality... you always have.

When you get lost along the way find a piece of paper or a notebook and write down what you're grateful for as well as what your dream is (remember to write your dream as though it has already happened). Write your dream on your bathroom mirror. Tape it to your phone or make it the lock screen image on your phone. Put it where you can see it. Keep it in front of you. Always ground yourself in gratitude, determination, positivity, and belief in yourself and you will land exactly where you are supposed to!

Finally, open your calendar and mark the date one year from today. In the notes, describe where you are on this day. Describe your situation and your dreams. In one year when you see that date approaching you will be amazed at the progress you have made.

Be courageous.

Be bold.

Be brave.

Be you.

Be known.

Now Go!

Final YouTube Assignment:
I want you to grab your phone and go to
www.adriennebulinski.com/guidebook
Look for the YouTube link titled "Jump"

If you enjoyed this guidebook we would be ever so

If you would leave us a review on Amazon!

Notes

Notes

Notes

About the Authors

Adrienne Bulinski

While Adrienne has lived in various corners of the country she is proud to be a Kansas native. Adrienne holds a BS in Journalism and Mass Communications as well as a Minor in Theatre from the University of Kansas. In 2005, she won the title of Miss Kansas, competing at Miss America 2006. Adrienne then joined the USO Show Troupe of Metropolitan New York, entertaining military troops and their families. In 2007 Adrienne derailed her professional entertainment career when she severed her foot from her leg due to a tragic horsing accident. Not giving into misfortune, Adrienne began performing again to prove statistics wrong. Today Adrienne has both of her feet and a newly installed ankle replacement. A woman of perseverance, Adrienne is also putting her journalism, marketing and public relations goals into action. Adrienne is the founder and director of Be Known, a marketing consulting and talent management company based in Arvada, CO. In her spare time, Adrienne enjoys being with her husband whether it is mountain biking, ski biking, watching TV, reading or cooking. She is also an avid writer. For daily inspiration join her on your favorite social platform @AdrienneBulinski

William V. (Bill) Anderson

Bill's favorite claims to fame come in the forms of husband, father, and papa. Aside from family life, Bill is a former Professor of Theatre Design at Louisiana State University (Geaux Tigers). He went on to produce conferences worldwide before he went back to his roots in Texas to save our nation's largest outdoor musical from bankruptcy. During his tenure as Executive Director he hired Adrienne as his Marketing Director and the rest is history. No matter what project or business Bill is developing he has spent his life trying to make things better for his family and anybody who he comes in contact with. He lives this guidebook: never backing down from a challenge, Bill has successfully built teams of good people to make great products. Bill is now the Creative Director of Be Known. You can read some of Bill's writing on Adrienne's website. He is based in Austin, TX and enjoys woodworking and getting ice cream with his granddaughters.

Also by Adrienne & Bill

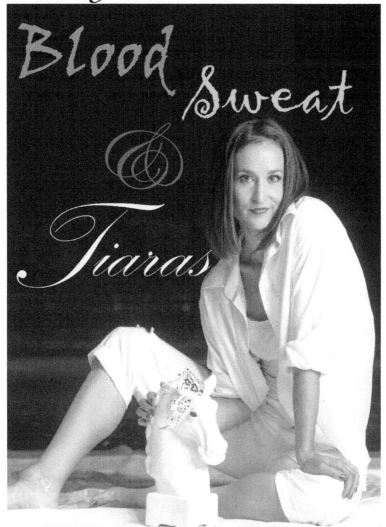

Blood Sweat & Tiaras

Adrienne Rosel Bulinski

edited with *William V. Anderson*

Made in the USA
Middletown, DE
16 October 2020